Basic
Level

Read on, Think on
考える基礎英語読本

Jonathan Lynch / Atsuko Yamamoto / Kanako Watanabe

SANSHUSHA

音声ダウンロード＆ストリーミングサービス（無料）のご案内

https://www.sanshusha.co.jp/onsei/isbn/9784384335019/

本書の音声データは、上記アドレスよりダウンロードおよびストリーミング再生ができます。ぜひご利用ください。

Download

Streaming

Preface

　読むことが楽しくなる理由は何でしょうか。それは人によって様々でしょう。短い読み物が好きな人は、長い読み物を退屈に感じるでしょう。自分に関係あることに興味がある人もいるでしょう。もちろん、面白いトピックについて読みたいと誰しも思っています。大学生向け英語のリーディング教材の問題点は、この3点（適切な長さか、学生に関係ある内容か、面白く読める内容か）に欠けていることにあると考え、この点に留意して、英語初級者がリーディングスキルの向上をめざすための動機付けになるような教科書を意図して作成しました。

　各ユニットでは若者にとって興味深い内容の短い読み物を取り扱っています。また各ユニットの単語レベルを頻出単語にしぼることにより、初級者でも読めるような英文にしました。学習者はむずかしくて長い英文に苦戦する代わりに有益な単語や表現、文法を学習することができます。

　最初にざっと英文に目を通し、2回目には英文の内容を深く考えながら読み進め（その際にはメモを取りながら読んでみるとよいでしょう）読み終わったら自分の言葉で英文を要約できるか確認してみましょう。3回目には音読してみるとよいでしょう。

　学習者の皆さんが各ユニットのトピックに触発されて英語へ興味を持ち、ひいては英語力向上をめざしていただけることを切に願っております。

Jonathan Lynch
Atsuko Yamamoto
Kanako Watanabe

Table of Contents

Unit 1 Noodles

Vocabulary Task 🎧 01-02

下記の語の意味を辞書で確認しましょう。

normal	somewhat	intensified	thus
aspect	participant	survey	location

空欄に上記の語を入れて意味の通る英文にしましょう。

1. The pain in my back _____ day by day.

2. Safety is a positive _____ of Japanese society.

3. We took a _____ of men under 60 for their opinions.

4. He will not be a _____ in this game.

5. It was very cold, and _____ we decided to buy another heater.

6. Her weight is _____ for her age.

7. This is a poor _____ for a noodle shop.

8. She is _____ lazy.

上記の語を本文中から見つけて○をつけましょう。

Reading

NOTES

1 Do you **slurp** noodles? For Japanese people, <u>it</u> is a completely normal thing, but for some foreign people coming to Japan, <u>it</u> is a somewhat surprising custom. Just by visiting a ramen shop in Japan, foreign tourists can learn about Japanese food culture.

2 Sometimes, foreign people ask their Japanese friends, "Why do Japanese people slurp noodles?" If you were asked this question, what would your answer be?

3 There might be three main reasons. First, noodles are served very hot. Slurping helps to cool the noodles down. Second, slurping **makes** the noodles more delicious. Taking in noodles and air at the same time intensifies the delicious flavors. Finally, slurping **lets** people around you know that you are enjoying the delicious noodles. <u>It</u> **conveys** a message that, "These noodles are delicious!" Thus <u>it</u> makes a great atmosphere for enjoying noodles.

4 However, is it acceptable to slurp noodles anywhere? Are there some situations <u>where</u> it is best to eat noodles quietly?

5 We asked some young Japanese people for their views on this question. Everybody said that, in a noodle shop or other restaurant in Japan, noisily slurping noodles is fine. Everybody should accept and enjoy <u>this</u> aspect of Japanese food culture.

6 However, in other places the situation is **less clear**. How about in an office **setting**? These days, many people eat a boxed lunch or a sandwich at their desk at lunchtime. If you worked in an office, would you slurp noodles at your desk? Some young people said yes, while others said no and a few said they would ask their **coworkers** for permission first.

7 How about on a **bullet train**? Many people eat all kinds of foods on bullet trains and <u>that</u> is normal, but is it OK to noisily slurp noodles there too? Most of the participants in our survey said that <u>they</u> probably would not slurp on the bullet train.

8 Perhaps the eating style depends on the location and the people surrounding us.

(322 words)

---

slurp
すする

make＋目的語＋形容詞
(目的語) を (形容詞の状態) にする
let＋目的語＋動詞の原形
(目的語) に (動詞の原形) させる
convey
伝える

less clear
よりあいまいである
setting
状況、環境、設定

coworker
同僚
bullet train
新幹線

Pair Work 下線部が何を指しているかパートナーと一緒に考えましょう。

True or False

本文の内容と一致すれば **T**（True）を、一致しなければ **F**（False）を記入しましょう。

( )1．These days, foreign people are coming to Japan in order to slurp noodles.

( )2．A visit to a ramen shop can teach foreign visitors about Japanese food culture.

( )3．There may be three explanations for the Japanese custom of slurping noodles.

( )4．Slurping noodles makes the noodles hotter.

( )5．All the Japanese people in the survey accept slurping noodles in restaurants.

( )6．Recently, people in offices often have lunch at their desks.

( )7．The people in the survey had various opinions about slurping noodles in an office.

( )8．In Japan, it is not permitted to slurp noodles on bullet trains.

Comprehension Questions

本文を読んで以下の質問に日本語で答えましょう。

1．外国人にとって驚くべき日本の習慣とは何ですか。

2．その驚くべき習慣の理由がいくつか述べられていますが、それらは何ですか。

3．日本の若者はその日本の習慣について、どのような意見を持っていますか。

Collocation

日本語をヒントに空欄を埋め意味の通る英文にしましょう。

1．If you eat ramen every day, you might **take**（　　　）too much salt.

「摂取する・飲み込む」

2．The students **asked**（　　　）information about the test. 「求める」

3．The expert gave his **views**（　　　）the election result. 「～についての見解」

4．**Some** people like watching TV, while（　　　　）like watching YouTube.

「～するものもあれば～するものもある」

5．Your test result **depends**（　　　）the amount of studying you do. 「～次第である」

Reading Summary

下記の日本語をヒントにして空欄に当てはまる語（1語とは限りません）を入れ、本文の要約を完成させましょう。必要なら辞書を使いましょう。

In Japan, people have a（　　　　　　　）to slurp noodles. There may be several （　　　　　　）for this. For example, slurping may communicate a feeling of （　　　　　　）. In addition, many people also think that it（　　　　　　）the taste of the noodles. Therefore, in Japan, an（　　　　　　）such as a ramen restaurant may be quite noisy. This may be surprising for foreign visitors to Japan. However, for Japanese people it is normal and in fact most visitors（　　　　　　） this aspect of Japanese food culture.（　　　　　　）, some Japanese people might （　　　　　　）from slurping noodles in certain locations. On the bullet train, for example, it is acceptable for（　　　　　　）to eat many types of foods but people slurping noodles are（　　　　　　）.

環境	理由	良くする	乗客	それにもかかわらず
珍しい	傾向	控える	満足	受け入れる

Grammar Point + Grammar Exercise

動名詞の働き

主語になる	<u>Slurping</u> helps to cool the noodles down.
目的語になる	Many foreign people also want to try <u>slurping</u>.

補語になる	My hobby is <u>jogging</u>.
前置詞の後に来る	He is fond of <u>eating</u>.

目的語を取る	<u>Playing tennis</u> is fun.
副詞（句）を伴う	Would you mind <u>walking slowly</u>?

動名詞を使用して次の和文を英語に訳しましょう。
1. 何も言わずに彼は部屋を出た。
2. 富士山に登ることは楽しい。
3. 百聞は一見にしかず。
4. ピアノを弾くことが好きだ。
5. 早足で歩くことが健康への鍵だ。

Unit 2 | Mysterious Object

Vocabulary Task 🎧 04-05

下記の語の意味を辞書で確認しましょう。

ancient	digging	formed	dimensional
object	suggestion	measure	estimated

空欄に上記の語を入れて意味の通る英文にしましょう。

1. What is that _____ on the table?

2. We _____ small groups in our English class to discuss various topics.

3. If I bake a cake, I use a digital scale to _____ the amount of sugar needed.

4. The mysterious Nazca Lines are _____ to be 2,000 years old.

5. The farmer is _____ in the field.

6. I agree with your _____. Let's go to the Italian restaurant!

7. Three-_____ printing is becoming popular these days.

8. Stonehenge is an _____ stone circle in England.

上記の語を本文中から見つけて○をつけましょう。

Reading

NOTES

1 Take a look at the object in the picture at the start of this unit. Can you guess what <u>it</u> is?

2 Do not worry if you cannot guess. Actually, nobody knows this object's true purpose. In fact, it may be difficult to find out because it is almost 2,000 years old.

3 This mysterious object is called a Roman **dodecahedron**. More than 100 of <u>these</u> have been found in European countries <u>which</u> were part of the ancient **Roman empire**. <u>Many</u> have been found by **archaeologists**, but <u>some</u> have also been discovered by ordinary people. <u>One</u> was found by a man digging in his garden in London, England.

4 A dodecahedron is a shape made by connecting pentagons to form a twelve-sided, three-dimensional object. Most of the Roman **dodecahedra** are made of **bronze**. <u>Each</u> of the twelve sides has a hole, but all the holes are of different sizes.

5 **What on earth** did the ancient Romans use these objects for? Over the years, many people have made suggestions.

6 One idea is that these dodecahedra were made to hold something, such as candles. Because there are different sized holes, candles of various sizes could be held safely.

7 Another idea is that <u>they</u> were used for measuring distances. By looking through a smaller hole and a larger hole at the same time, the distance to a **remote** object could be estimated.

8 More recently, some people have suggested that the dodecahedra were used for knitting. One man used a **replica** of a dodecahedron to knit a simple woolen glove. He made a video and uploaded it to YouTube. It is very interesting to watch.

9 There may be many other simpler explanations. Perhaps these objects were used in a children's game. Players threw small stones and tried to get <u>them</u> in one of the holes.

10 Can you think of a use for a Roman dodecahedron? Your guess is **as** good **as** anybody's!

(315 words)

dodecahedron	十二面体
Roman empire	ローマ帝国
archaeologist	考古学者
dodecahedra	十二面体 (複数形)
bronze	青銅
what on earth ～?	いったいぜんたい何 ～？
remote	遠く離れた
replica	複製品
as＋形容詞＋as～	～と同じくらい

 Pair Work　下線部が何を指しているかパートナーと一緒に考えましょう。

True or False

本文の内容と一致すれば **T** (True) を、一致しなければ **F** (False) を記入しましょう。

( ) 1．The objects mentioned in the story are nearly 2,000 years old.

( ) 2．Roman dodecahedra have only been found in England.

( ) 3．A dodecahedron is an object with twelve pentagon-shaped sides.

( ) 4．Roman dodecahedra are all made of metal.

( ) 5．A dodecahedron might have held candles of various shapes and sizes.

( ) 6．Dodecahedra may have been used to estimate area.

( ) 7．The real purpose of these objects can be checked on YouTube.

( ) 8．Children in Roman times used them for school work.

Comprehension Questions

本文を読んで以下の質問に日本語で答えましょう。

1．この物体の形を具体的に説明しなさい。

2．この物体はどこで何体発見されていますか。

3．この物体の考えられる目的は何であると述べられていますか。

Collocation

日本語をヒントに空欄を埋め意味の通る英文にしましょう。

1．Please ( ) **a look** at this photograph. 「〜を見てみる」

2．( ) **fact**, I have never been to another country. 「実際に」

3．This necklace is **made** ( ) 24-karat gold. 「で作られている」

4．The **distance** ( ) Osaka from here is about 400 kilometers. 「〜への距離」

5．Let's **think** ( ) some good ways to protect the environment. 「〜を考える」

Reading Summary

下記の日本語をヒントにして空欄に当てはまる語（1語とは限りません）を入れ、本文の要約を完成させましょう。必要なら辞書を使いましょう。

Over 100 (　　　　　) objects have been found in European countries. Each of these objects is in the shape of a dodecahedron and most (　　　　　) metal. They were used by ancient people about 2,000 years ago, but their true (　　　　　) is a mystery. Many different (　　　　　) have been proposed about their role. Some people have suggested that they were (　　　　　). They might have been very (　　　　　) because they could hold different sizes of candle. Another proposal is that they were used to measure distance. One person thinks that they were used for making (　　　　　). He even tried to (　　　　　) gloves with a replica dodecahedron. (　　　　　) they had an even simpler purpose, as objects in children's games. The fact is, (　　　　　) knows their true purpose.

説	便利な	ろうそく立て	たぶん	編む
誰も〜ない	服	目的	同じような	〜で作られている

Grammar Point + Grammar Exercise

受動態

be 動詞は主語の人称と数に一致する。時制にも注意しよう。
助動詞がある場合は 助動詞＋be＋過去分詞となる。

This mysterious object <u>is called</u> a Roman dodecahedron.
They <u>have been found</u> in European countries.
Candles of various sizes <u>could be held</u> safely.
One <u>was found</u> by a man digging in his garden in London, England.
These objects <u>were used</u> in a children's game.

受動態を使用して次の和文を英語に訳しましょう。
1．ランチがただ今調理されている。
2．一晩中われわれは働かされた。
3．これは後ほど処理される予定だ。
4．離れた物体までの距離が推測できる。
5．これらは青銅でできている。

Unit 3 | Baskin-Robbins

Vocabulary Task

07-08

下記の語の意味を辞書で確認しましょう。

annual	available	concept	consumption
founded	indicate	items	selection

空欄に上記の語を入れて意味の通る英文にしましょう。

1. My mother has a list of ten _____ to buy at the department store.

2. _____ tax will increase at the end of this year.

3. Her _____ income is fifty thousand dollars.

4. Can you _____ where your school is located?

5. The _____ of learning is difficult to define.

6. That store offers a large _____ of wine.

7. Our manager is not _____ right now.

8. Our company was _____ several years ago.

上記の語を本文中から見つけて○をつけましょう。

Reading

NOTES

1 Japan is a great place to be if you like ice cream.

2 Foreign visitors to Japan are often surprised by **the variety of** delicious and unique Japanese ice creams. Matcha-flavored ice cream, for example, is a **must-try** item for many foreign tourists.

3 Japanese people themselves eat a lot of ice cream. In the world rankings, Japan is 17th for annual ice-cream consumption **per person**. <u>That</u> is ahead of some countries famous for producing sweet things, **including** France, Belgium and Switzerland.

4 Specialty ice-cream shops are popular in Japan, too. Among <u>these</u>, the chain called "Thirty One Ice Cream" is probably the most **well known**. However, if a Japanese person says "Let's go to Thirty One!" to a foreign friend, that friend will probably be **confused**. In most countries, "Thirty One Ice Cream" is called "Baskin-Robbins."

5 Now famous all over the world, Baskin-Robbins was founded in California by Mr. Baskin and Mr. Robbins. Both men **owned** separate ice cream stores <u>which</u> <u>they</u> **merged** to make the first Baskin-Robbins store in 1953.

6 Baskin-Robbins is famous for <u>its</u> "31 flavors" slogan. The concept is that customers can enjoy a different flavor every day of the month... 31 days, 31 flavors. <u>This</u> means that, in just one month, you can have fun tasting many delicious flavors.

7 If truth be told, it seems unlikely that people will eat Baskin-Robbins ice cream every day for a month. However, the basic point is clear — there are a lot of flavors to try! A wide selection is part of the appeal of Baskin-Robbins.

8 In Japan, customers are lucky. There are actually 32 flavors, divided into 21 standard flavors and 11 seasonal flavors. Sales data indicate that the top standard flavors are: in third place, Strawberry Cheesecake, in second place, Caramel Ribbon and in the top position, Popping Shower... a best-selling flavor <u>that</u> is only available in Japan.

9 Whether with family, with friends or just as a treat for yourself, dropping by Baskin-Robbins is a great way to add a little happiness to the day.

(335 words)

the variety of ～
～の多様性

must-try
外せない

per person
一人につき

including ～
～を含めて

well known
よく知られた
confused
困惑する

own
所有する
merge
合併する

 Pair Work 下線部が何を指しているかパートナーと一緒に考えましょう。

True or False

本文の内容と一致すれば **T** (True) を、一致しなければ **F** (False) を記入しましょう。

( ) 1. Most foreign visitors to Japan avoid matcha-flavored ice cream.

( ) 2. Japanese people consume more ice-cream per person than French people.

( ) 3. "Thirty One Ice Cream" has a different name in countries outside Japan.

( ) 4. Baskin-Robbins was established in California.

( ) 5. The "31 flavors" slogan is connected to famous cities in America.

( ) 6. In Japan, there are more seasonal flavors than standard flavors.

( ) 7. Caramel Ribbon is the most popular flavor in Japan.

( ) 8. Popping Shower flavor is available worldwide.

Unit 3

Comprehension Questions

本文を読んで以下の質問に日本語で答えましょう。

1. 店名の「サーティワン」にはどんな意味がありますか。

2. 外国人が日本人の友人に「サーティワン アイスクリームに行こう」と誘われたときに戸惑う理由は何ですか。

3. 日本におけるフレーバー 32 種類の内訳を説明しましょう。

Collocation

日本語をヒントに空欄を埋め意味の通る英文にしましょう。

1. He finished the race **ahead (   )** me. 「～の前に」

2. Japan is **famous (   )** its trains that run on time. 「～で有名な」

3. The pizza was **divided (   )** eight pieces for the children. 「～に分けられる」

4. I **dropped (   )** my friend's house on the way to the shops. 「立ち寄る」

5. This language game will **add** some fun **(   )** the lesson. 「～に加える」

Reading Summary

下記の日本語をヒントにして空欄に当てはまる語（1語とは限りません）を入れ、本文の要約を完成させましょう。必要なら辞書を使いましょう。

Ice cream is popular in Japan and unique flavors of Japanese ice cream are enjoyed by both Japanese people and foreign visitors. One major chain of (　　　　　　　) ice-cream shops (　　　　　　) in Japan is called "Thirty One Ice Cream." In other countries, this chain is called "Baskin-Robbins." It (　　　　　　　) in America (　　　　　) ago after two men (　　　　　　　) their ice cream stores. The 31 concept is (　　　　　　) days in the month. Customers can enjoy a different flavor every day of the month. Being able to (　　　　　) many flavors is an important part of this chain's marketing strategy. Japanese Baskin-Robbins shops (　　　　　　) standard flavors and (　　　　　　) flavors. The biggest-selling flavor is Popping Shower which is not (　　　　　) outside Japan.

新たに始まった	合併した	～から選ぶ	～に関連した	季節の
数十年	提供する	手に入る	見つかる	専門、特製品

Grammar Point + Grammar Exercise

不定詞の働き

名詞の働きをする

I want to eat ice cream.

形容詞の働きをする

Japan is a great place to be if you like ice cream.

副詞の働きをする

They merged their companies to make the first Baskin-Robbins store in 1953.

不定詞を使用して次の和文を英語に訳しましょう。

1．トライできるたくさんのフレーバーがあります。
2．私はすべてのフレーバーをトライしたい。
3．彼はすべてのフレーバーをトライするために毎日そのアイスクリーム店に行く。
4．すべてのフレーバーをトライすることは不可能だ。
5．どのフレーバーを選んだらよいかわからない。

Unit 4 Dealing with "Claimers"

Vocabulary Task

🎧 10-11

下記の語の意味を辞書で確認しましょう。

complain	incidents	quit	media
unreasonable	staff	apologized	resolved

空欄に上記の語を入れて意味の通る英文にしましょう。

1．A lot of _____ made me think he was a criminal.

2．The problem will be _____ soon.

3．Customers often _____ about the slow service at that restaurant.

4．Tom _____ his job and went abroad to study.

5．The _____ gave a lot of attention to the politician's marriage.

6．The student _____ to the teacher for being late for class.

7．That's an _____ price for a small purse.

8．The office _____ goes on a trip every summer.

上記の語を本文中から見つけて○をつけましょう。

19

Reading

NOTES

1 It was just a normal Saturday for Fumito Ishibashi. He arrived at the shopping **mall** at 9:30 a.m. for his part-time job in the café. It was a busy day, as usual.

2 Around lunchtime, a customer ordered a mango **smoothie** that Fumito had never made before. Unfortunately, while making it, Fumito got it wrong. "I made a mistake," he **said to himself**, but his voice must have been louder than he thought. The customer heard him and then got very angry.

3 "You've made me feel bad," shouted the customer, a middle-aged woman. "I don't want that smoothie any more." The woman left the shop, still complaining loudly.

4 Fumito regretted the incident, but it was not over. The customer later called the shopping mall and complained a lot more. **In the end**, both the manager of the café and the manager of the shopping mall scolded Fumito. He felt so bad that he later quit his job.

5 The Japanese media call such customers "claimers." However, this word is not used in English. We need a longer expression, such as "a customer who makes unreasonable **complaints**."

6 So what should staff do? The most important thing is to stay calm. The staff themselves should never get angry. First, apologize politely and try to resolve the problem quickly. In many cases, it may be necessary to call the manager, especially if the person complaining seems to be escalating the situation.

7 In the case above, Fumito offered to remake the smoothie, but this did not satisfy the customer. Later he **remarked**, "I learned a lot from this incident. Above all, I learned that there are some very unreasonable people in the world. Even if we apologize for a mistake, they will not accept it. We have to be very careful when dealing with them."

(299 words)

mall
ショッピングセンター

smoothie
スムージー

say to oneself
独り言を言う

in the end
最後に

complaint
不満、苦情、文句

remark
言う

 **Pair Work** 下線部が何を指しているかパートナーと一緒に考えましょう。

True or False

本文の内容と一致すれば **T** (True) を、一致しなければ **F** (False) を記入しましょう。

( ) 1. Fumito had a full-time job.

( ) 2. The customer ordered a beverage.

( ) 3. The problem occurred due to Fumito's mistake.

( ) 4. The customer was angry about the slow service.

( ) 5. Fumito was scolded by more than one person.

( ) 6. The expression "claimer" is not commonly used in English.

( ) 7. Staff should ignore angry customers if possible.

( ) 8. The experience taught something to Fumito.

Comprehension Questions

本文を読んで以下の質問に日本語で答えましょう。

1. 石橋フミトが仕事を辞めた理由は何ですか。

2. 日本語の「クレーマー」は英語では何といいますか。

3. クレーマーの対処法は何ですか。

Collocation

日本語をヒントに空欄を埋め意味の通る英文にしましょう。

1. I woke up at 7 o'clock **as (**). 「いつものように」

2. If you **get it (**) next time, you will be fired. 「やりそこなう」

3. I do **not** watch TV ( ) **more**. I prefer using the Internet. 「もはや〜でない」

4. He often ( ) **a complaint** to his neighbors about loud noises.

「苦情を言う」

5. **Above (**), we should have good manners in public. 「何よりも」

21

Reading Summary

下記の日本語をヒントにして空欄に当てはまる語（1語とは限りません）を入れ、本文の要約を完成させましょう。必要なら辞書を使いましょう。

Fumito Ishibashi had a problem with a customer. The problem was (　　　　　　　　) Fumito's mistake, but the customer seemed to overreact. She started shouting and later telephoned Fumito's workplace to (　　　　　　　) some more. (　　　　　　), Fumito was (　　　　　　) his managers and eventually (　　　　　　) his job. In Japan, a special expression has become common to describe such customers: "claimers." In English, there is no such (　　　　　　), so a longer phrase such as "customers who complain a lot" might be used. It is not easy to (　　　　　) such customers by any means. (　　　　　　) must stay calm, try to find a (　　　　　　) and get help from the manager if necessary. Sometimes it may not be possible to satisfy the customer's (　　　　　　) demands. Nevertheless, dealing with "claimers" can teach us something.

解決策	結果として	～が原因で	職員 / 従業員	～に対処する
～に叱られる	文句を言う	表現	理不尽な	辞めた

Grammar Point + Grammar Exercise

形容詞の働き

名詞を修飾する　　It was just a <u>normal</u> Saturday.
主格補語となる　　The woman was very <u>angry</u>.
目的格補語となる　You've made me very <u>happy</u>.

主な形容詞の接尾辞

norm<u>al</u>　fortun<u>ate</u>　unreason<u>able</u>　use<u>ful</u>　art<u>istic</u>　obv<u>ious</u>　act<u>ive</u>　health<u>y</u>

和文を参照して（　　）内に適切な動詞、または形容詞を入れて英文を完成させましょう。

1. Going to a gym (　　　　　) him (　　　　　).
   ジムに行くことで彼は健康でいられる。

2. Some customers (　　　　　) (　　　　　　) complaints.
   顧客によっては常軌を逸した文句を言う人もいる。

3. He (　　　　　) a customer very (　　　　　). 彼は顧客を大変満足させた。

4. The customer was (　　　　　) and (　　　　　) a lot.
   その顧客は怒って文句を大いに言った。

5. The guidelines for serving customers (　　　　　) very (　　　　　).
   顧客対応のためのガイドラインは大いに役に立つ。

Unit 5 | Haunted Campus?

Vocabulary Task

🎧 13-14

下記の語の意味を辞書で確認しましょう。

occasionally	experience	corridor	security
finally	descend	fright	approach

空欄に上記の語を入れて意味の通る英文にしましょう。

1. After walking around for some time, we _____ found Tom's house.

2. My family gives me a feeling of _____.

3. This _____ has an emergency exit near the elevator.

4. I _____ go to the movie theater. Maybe two or three times a year.

5. We often _____ earthquakes in Japan.

6. Be careful when you _____ that dog. It bites.

7. The plane will _____ in a few minutes.

8. The big spider gave me a _____.

上記の語を本文中から見つけて○をつけましょう。

Reading

NOTES

1 Mark Adams is an English teacher at a university in Tokyo. He likes his job, his students and his office—a small room on the top floor of an old building, called the "4th Building."

2 Students have occasionally told Mark that the 4th Building is **haunted**. He did not believe that, until he started to experience strange things there himself.

> haunted
> 幽霊の出る

3 The first incident happened when Mark was working late one evening. It was after 11 o'clock and the whole building was dark. He heard footsteps in the corridor. "It's the security guard," thought Mark. The footsteps came closer and closer and finally stopped, **right outside** his door. Nobody knocked. He stood up, moved to the door and quickly opened it. There was nobody there. The dark corridor was empty.

> right (outside ～)
> ちょうど

4 Another time, he was working late again. After he had finished, he got ready to go home and took the **trash** bag with him. He wanted to use the restroom at the end of the corridor, so he placed the trash bag on the floor, in front of the restroom door. While inside, he was sure he heard a noise from the dark corridor. When he came out, he found that the trash bag had moved about two meters.

> trash
> ゴミ

5 Usually the experiences happened late at night. One experience happened again and again. After finishing work, he **would** take the elevator from his floor, the fifth floor, to the ground floor. Inside the elevator he would press the button marked "1," and the elevator would descend. However, **for no reason**, the elevator would often stop at the third floor. The door would open, but nobody was there. Just a dark corridor.

> would
> ～したものだ

> for no reason
> なぜかしら

6 One time, he got a fright on the **ground floor**. A dark **figure** suddenly approached him **from the shadows**. Fortunately, it was just the security guard, an old man. Mark made a greeting and **was about to leave when** the guard said in Japanese, "Professor Adams, it's best not to work late in this building... strange things appear here. And please... never visit the third floor at night."

(346 words)

> ground floor
> 1 階
> figure
> 人影、人物
> from the shadows
> 陰から、暗闇から
> was about to leave when
> 出ようとしたとき

 Pair Work　下線部が何を指しているかパートナーと一緒に考えましょう。

True or False

本文の内容と一致すれば **T**（True）を、一致しなければ **F**（False）を記入しましょう。

（　）1．Mark Adams teaches English in Japan.

（　）2．Students at the university believe that the 4th Building is haunted.

（　）3．Mark sometimes works late.

（　）4．He once heard footsteps inside a classroom.

（　）5．An item seemed to move mysteriously from one spot to another.

（　）6．Sometimes the elevator would stop mysteriously.

（　）7．The security guard helped Mark to find the exit.

（　）8．The security guard advised him not to leave his room at night.

Comprehension Questions

本文を読んで以下の質問に日本語で答えましょう。

1．マーク・アダムスが経験した不可思議な出来事はいくつ述べられていますか。

2．不可思議な出来事の内容をそれぞれ説明してみましょう。

3．マーク・アダムスが不可思議な体験を回避するにはどうしたらよいでしょうか。

Collocation

日本語をヒントに空欄を埋め意味の通る英文にしましょう。

1．He **got**（　　　　　）**to** go home after finishing his work. 「～する準備ができている」

2．You can use the bathroom **at the**（　　　　）**of** the corridor. 「～のつきあたりに」

3．She sits（　　　）**front of** me in this class. 「～の前に」

4．Cars must **stop**（　　　）the red light. 「～で止まる」

5．The students had to（　　　　　）**a greeting** to their teacher. 「挨拶する」

Reading Summary

下記の日本語をヒントにして空欄に当てはまる語（1語とは限りません）を入れ、本文の要約を完成させましょう。必要なら辞書を使いましょう。

At the university where he worked, there were (　　　　　) that the 4th Building was haunted, but Mark Adams did not believe them. (　　　　　), he had some experiences in that building which seemed difficult to explain. (　　　　　), he heard strange footsteps in the corridor outside his office. When he checked, there was nobody in the corridor. On another occasion, a bag of trash that he left in the corridor moved to a different spot (　　　　　) he was using the restroom. (　　　　　), he experienced a strange episode in the elevator. (　　　　　), the same thing happened (　　　　　). He pressed the (　　　　　) for the ground floor but, on the way, the elevator would stop at the third floor. The doors would open, but nobody got in the elevator and nobody was in the corridor. An old (　　　　　) warned Mark not to work late in the building because, he said, strange things (　　　　　) appear at night time.

〜の間	うわさ	警備員	さらに	〜しがちであった
しかし	実際のところ	数回	まず初めに	ボタン

Grammar Point + Grammar Exercise

頻度を表す副詞の位置

100% ←　　　　　　　　　　　　　　　　　　　　　　　　→ 0%

| always | usually | often | sometimes | rarely | never |

be 動詞の後　　Mark was <u>always</u> late for class.
一般動詞の前　The experiences <u>usually</u> happened late at night.
助動詞の後　　The security guard would <u>sometimes</u> patrol late at night.

（　）内の語を並べ替えて意味の通る英文にしましょう。

1. I (get, at, usually, up, seven).
2. (younger, watch, people, rarely, TV).
3. Strange (appear, night, things, sometimes, at).
4. (very, you, always, are, welcome).
5. We can (go, concert, sometimes, to, a).

Unit 6

Solo Artists Are More Popular

Unit 6

Vocabulary Task

🎧 16-17

下記の語の意味を辞書で確認しましょう。

evolved	trend	performer	traditional
common	minor	expense	furthermore

空欄に上記の語を入れて意味の通る英文にしましょう。

1. Candy is expensive; _____, it is bad for your health.

2. One _____ is that many young people do not watch TV.

3. Sato is probably the most _____ family name in Japan.

4. We believe that birds _____ from dinosaurs.

5. The haiku is a _____ form of literature in Japan.

6. Lady Gaga is a popular _____ and songwriter.

7. This has a _____ effect on the economy.

8. We must calculate the _____ of renovating the office.

上記の語を本文中から見つけて○をつけましょう。

27

Reading

 18

1 Popular music is always evolving. New styles of music and new fashions appear. Some artists become popular for just a short time, while others become **long-term** stars.

2 Internationally, there is one trend <u>that</u> has become **noticeable** recently. Almost all of the most popular musicians are now solo artists. Bruno Mars, Ed Sheeran, Ariana Grande, Taylor Swift... these solo performers and others like them are the **big sellers** worldwide.

3 So what happened to the bands?

4 One reason must be the decline in popularity of rock music. The traditional rock **combo** of vocals, lead guitar, rhythm guitar, bass and drums is much less common these days. Rather than being a central part of popular music, rock is now a minor **genre**. Of course, there are still rock fans, but their numbers are lower now. **Indeed**, for many young people, rock is the music <u>that</u> their parents or even grandparents liked.

5 In addition, pop music has become **digitalized**. <u>This</u> might be a very good thing. These days, anyone can make incredible music with just <u>their</u> laptop and "**digital audio workstation**" software such as **Ableton Live** or **FL Studio**. Digital instruments are included with the software, so **wannabe musicians** can do everything <u>themselves</u>, without the expense of buying musical instruments.

6 Furthermore, because popular music has become digitalized, a **charismatic** vocalist is the only human performer <u>that</u> is needed. Thanks to the software, drum, guitar and keyboard tracks can be created by computer.

7 And of course, one more important aspect is the impact of rap and hip-hop on popular music. These days, the most popular music in America and worldwide is produced by rappers, hip-hop artists and DJs, <u>who</u> mainly perform as solo artists. Because <u>they</u> strongly influence other performers, <u>they</u> have moved popular music away from band-based styles towards solo-artist styles.

(297 words)

long-term	長期の
noticeable	顕著な
big seller	人気商品
combo	小編成の楽団
genre	ジャンル
indeed	確かに（強調する場合に使う）
digitalized	デジタル化した
digital audio workstation	デジタルで録音、編集、ミキシング、編曲などの作業が出来るシステム
Ableton Live	（エイブルトンライブ）
FL Studio	（エフエルスタジオ）どちらもデジタルで音声や曲の録音、編集ができるシステム
wannabe musician	ミュージシャンになりたい人
charismatic	カリスマ的な

Pair Work 下線部が何を指しているかパートナーと一緒に考えましょう。

True or False

本文の内容と一致すれば **T** (True) を、一致しなければ **F** (False) を記入しましょう。

(　) 1 ． Solo artists have declined in popularity recently.

(　) 2 ． Bruno Mars is the most popular artist in the world.

(　) 3 ． Rock music had become less popular, but now is becoming popular again.

(　) 4 ． Thanks to software, it is easy for anyone to make music.

(　) 5 ． Besides the software, users must also buy musical instruments.

(　) 6 ． Because the software can do everything, a vocalist is no longer required.

(　) 7 ． Rap and hip-hop have been influenced by the rock genre.

(　) 8 ． Rappers and hip-hop artists tend to perform as solo artists.

Comprehension Questions

本文を読んで以下の質問に日本語で答えましょう。

1 ． 音楽界の最近のトレンドは何ですか。

2 ． ロックは現在の多くの若者にとってどのような存在ですか。

3 ． ポップミュージックがデジタル化された結果、どのようなことが起きていますか。

Unit 6

Collocation

日本語をヒントに空欄を埋め意味の通る英文にしましょう。

1 ． There is a **decline** (　 　) the number of young people in Japan. 「〜の減少」

2 ． **Rather** (　 　 　) bad news, that is actually a good thing. 「〜よりむしろ」

3 ． **Thanks** (　 　) the great vocalist, the band became successful. 「〜のおかげで」

4 ． The **impact** of the Internet (　 　) shopping habits has been big. 「〜への影響」

5 ． The iPad has **moved** reading **away from** paper books (　 　 　 　) ebooks.

「〜から〜へ動かす」

Reading Summary

下記の日本語をヒントにして空欄に当てはまる語（1語とは限りません）を入れ、本文の要約を完成させましょう。必要なら辞書を使いましょう。

There are many (　　　　　　　) in popular music. Among these, one recent trend is that bands have become (　　　　　　) and solo artists are now (　　　　　　) performers. Several different (　　　　　　) might explain this trend. Firstly, rock music bands are (　　　　　　) these days. Although rock still has many fans, this (　　　　　　) may seem to be somewhat old-fashioned for young people. Secondly, music production is now a digital process. In fact, young people can produce their own music easily by using computers and special software. This (　　　　　　) that they do not have to (　　　　　　) musical instruments. They can do everything by themselves and only a vocalist is needed because all the other (　　　　　　) can be produced by the software. One more (　　　　　　) is that rap and hip-hop music are probably the most popular genres these days. Because they tend to be performed by solo artists, these genres are pushing mainstream music towards solo-artist styles.

〜を意味する	傾向	形式・ジャンル	部分	購入する
最も人気のある	要素	より人気のない	より普通でない	理由

Grammar Point + Grammar Exercise

比較級、最上級の強め方 / 劣等比較

Solo stars are now **much** <u>more popular than</u> bands.
Solo artists are **by far** <u>the most popular</u> musicians recently.

劣等比較 less + 原級 + than 〜 の形で「〜より劣る、より少ない、〜ほどでない」ということを表します。

次の英文を日本語に訳しましょう。

1．He is by far the best musician in the world.
2．Rock is much simpler than people think.
3．This book is much the best.
4．This car is less expensive than the previous one.
5．This air conditioner was less effective than a new model.

Unit 7　Headphones

Vocabulary Task

🎧 19-20

下記の語の意味を辞書で確認しましょう。

managed	priority	area	technologies
tends	generation	purchase	hygienic

空欄に上記の語を入れて意味の通る英文にしましょう。

1. Tom finally _____ to finish his work.

2. The doctor's _____ of medicine is cancer.

3. You should compare prices at different stores before you _____ an air conditioner.

4. Mary _____ to be shy.

5. The kitchen is very _____. It is cleaned every day.

6. Car manufacturers are developing fuel-saving _____.

7. People of grandfather's _____ did not have television when they were children.

8. Fire engines have _____ over other vehicles.

上記の語を本文中から見つけて○をつけましょう。

Reading

 21

NOTES

1 Besides a smartphone, what is the most important item for young people these days? If they manage to save some money, what do <u>they</u> really want to buy?

2 For many youngsters, **it seems that** a good set of headphones is a priority.

3 **In fact**, <u>this</u> is an area where technology is developing rapidly. New and better models are appearing **all the time**. And because <u>they</u> tend to wear out quickly, many young people **upgrade** <u>their</u> headphones every year or two.

4 If members of the older generation visit an **electronics store**, they might be amazed by the choice of headphones.

5 When purchasing headphones, the first thing to decide is the type. Which do you prefer: **over ear**, **in ear** or **earbuds**? Do you want **wired** or **wireless** headphones?

6 For people <u>who</u> do not worry about weight so much, over-ear headphones are a popular choice. <u>They</u> give great sound quality and also have another advantage—<u>they</u> might keep your ears warm in winter!

7 In-ear headphones are probably the most popular type. <u>They</u> come with **silicone ear tips** <u>that</u> fit inside the **ear canal**. <u>They</u> are small and convenient although, in public, users must be careful because this type can block out all other sounds.

8 Earbuds are also small. <u>They</u> fit inside the ear but do not go inside the ear canal. An advantage of this type is that they are easy to clean and hygienic. A disadvantage might be that sound can leak out easily.

9 All of these types are now available as wireless models, <u>which</u> connect to smartphones by **bluetooth**. They are great technology, but some problems can occur. For example, some types can fall out of your ear and drop on the floor. That can be embarrassing inside a crowded train. In addition, people sometimes forget to switch on the bluetooth connection and, as a result, music suddenly **blasts out** from the smartphone speaker.

(312 words)

---

it seems that 主語＋動詞
that 以下のように思える

in fact
もっとはっきり言えば

all the time
いつも

upgrade
品質を良くする

electronics store
電子製品店

over ear
オーバーイア型

in ear
インイア型

earbud
耳の穴差し込み型

wired
有線の

wireless
無線の

silicone
シリコン

ear tips
イヤーチップ

ear canal
外耳道

bluetooth
ブルートゥース（無線通信技術）

blast out
大きい音を出す

Pair Work 下線部が何を指しているかパートナーと一緒に考えましょう。

True or False

本文の内容と一致すれば **T** (True) を、一致しなければ **F** (False) を記入しましょう。

( ) 1．Headphones are not so important for young people.

( ) 2．Many young people replace their headphones frequently.

( ) 3．When buying new headphones, we must consider the type we want.

( ) 4．Over-ear headphones are the lightest type of headphones.

( ) 5．In-ear headphones are placed inside the ear canal.

( ) 6．Earbuds are similar to in-ear headphones but do not go inside the ear canal.

( ) 7．It is possible that the sound from earbuds might bother other people.

( ) 8．Wireless headphones might become available in the future.

Comprehension Questions

本文を読んで以下の質問に日本語で答えましょう。

1．何種類のヘッドフォンについて述べられていますか。

2．それぞれのヘッドフォンの特徴は何ですか。

3．無線のヘッドフォンの問題点とは何ですか。

Collocation

日本語をヒントに空欄を埋め意味の通る英文にしましょう。

1．He **wore** (　　　　　) his sneakers after using them for a long time. 「履き古す」

2．Tea or coffee **comes** (　　　　　) this meal. 「～を備えた」

3．The news about the scandal **leaked** (　　　　). 「漏れる」

4．Wireless speakers can **connect** (　　　) mobile devices. 「～につながる」

5．Can I **switch** (　　　) the heater? It's cold in here. 「つける」

Reading Summary

下記の日本語をヒントにして空欄に当てはまる語（1語とは限りません）を入れ、本文の要約を完成させましょう。必要なら辞書を使いましょう。

Buying a good set of headphones is an important （　　　　　　　） for many young people these days. （　　　　　　　） the past, there is a wide range of headphone models （　　　　　　　） today. Headphones can be （　　　　　　　） various categories （　　　　　　　） over ear, in ear or earbuds. Each type has （　　　　　　　） and users must decide which type suits them best. Over-ear headphones （　　　　　　　） be larger and heavier but have excellent sound quality. They might also act as ear warmers in winter. （　　　　　　　）, for people who like smaller convenient headphones, in-ear types or earbuds might be the best choice. In-ear headphones have special tips that go inside the ear canal. Earbuds rest inside the ear but might have a problem with sound （　　　　　　　）, especially for people who listen to music at high volumes. Wireless headphones are becoming common but we must be careful not to let them （　　　　　　　） to the ground.

一方	買い物	～の傾向がある	手に入る	～と比べて
落ちる	～に分類される	～のような	漏れ	利点

Grammar Point + Grammar Exercise

つなぎの言葉①

理由を表す

<u>Because</u> they wear out quickly, people upgrade them often.
They just rest inside the ear, <u>so</u> they may be a good choice for some people.
They just rest inside the ear; <u>therefore</u>, they may be a good choice for some people.

対立を表す

<u>Although</u> they fit inside the ear, they do not go inside the ear canal.
They fit inside the ear, <u>but</u> they do not go inside the ear canal.
They fit inside the ear; <u>however</u>, they do not go inside the ear canal.

上記のつなぎの言葉を（　）内に入れて、英文を完成させましょう。

1. He was sick, （　　　　　　　） he went to school.　病気だったが、学校に行った。
2. （　　　　　　　） he is young, he is very dependable.　若いが頼りがいがある。
3. The weather was fine; （　　　　　　　）, the game was cancelled.
　天候は良かったが、試合は中止になった。
4. （　　　　　　　） the weather was bad, the picnic was postponed.
　天候が悪かったので、ピクニックは延期された。
5. He studied hard; （　　　　　　　）, he passed the test.
　一生懸命勉強したのでテストに合格した。

Unit 8 Where Did the Moon Come From?

Vocabulary Task

🎧 22-23

下記の語の意味を辞書で確認しましょう。

phenomena	occur	hypothesis	created
scenario	eventually	evidence	analyze

空欄に上記の語を入れて意味の通る英文にしましょう。

1．Scientists proposed a new _____ to explain time travel.

2．She used a computer to _____ the data.

3．Living things will _____ die.

4．The musician _____ a new song.

5．Tornadoes and hurricanes are examples of weather _____.

6．_____ of life on Mars has not been found yet.

7．Supermoons _____ about twice a year.

8．What is the most likely _____ if a typhoon strikes this area?

上記の語を本文中から見つけて○をつけましょう。

Reading

🎧 24

NOTES

1 If you are a dreamer, perhaps you enjoy **stargazing**.

2 For people <u>who</u> like to dream, imagine things and find escape from daily life, looking up at the night sky and gazing at the Moon and stars is a nice way to spend time.

3 Sometimes we can see mysterious phenomena, such as a **blood moon** <u>that</u> occurs during a **lunar eclipse**.

4 But have you ever looked at the Moon and wondered where <u>it</u> came from? Why are we blessed with such a beautiful object in the night sky?

5 Actually, scientists are not sure. The Moon <u>that</u> we see now was made billions of years ago, and so scientists can only make a hypothesis about its origins.

6 Basically, there are four main ideas: 1) an **early planet** split <u>itself</u> into the Earth and Moon; 2) the Moon was an object **captured by** the Earth's **gravity**; 3) the Earth and Moon were made from dust and rocks at the same time; 4) another planet **smashed into** the young Earth and created the Moon.

7 Among these, many scientists think that scenario number 4 is the most likely.

8 It is interesting to think about <u>this</u> scenario. First, let's note that the young Earth has an informal name… it is called **Gaia**. Scientists think that there was another planet near to Gaia, called **Theia**. It was smaller than Gaia and <u>its</u> **orbit** brought <u>it</u> closer and closer, until finally the two **planets** smashed together.

9 Scientists propose that, after the **collision**, Theia was mainly absorbed into Gaia. However, a lot of rocks and dust were **ejected** into space. These **started orbiting** the young Earth and eventually **coalesced** to make the Moon.

10 Evidence for this **theory** can be found by analyzing moon rocks. Scientists have some rocks from the Apollo moon landings 50 years ago, but <u>they</u> need more. Perhaps it is time for humans to visit the Moon again!

(312 words)

---

stargaze
星を眺める

blood moon
皆既月食の際、月が赤く色づいて見える自然現象
lunar eclipse
月食

early planet
原始惑星
captured by
（重力に）捕らえられた～
gravity 引力
smash into
～に激突する

Gaia
ガイア（ギリシャ神話の地母神に由来）
Theia
ティア（ギリシャ神話の月の女神の母親に由来）
orbit 軌道
planet 惑星
collision 衝突
eject 放出する
started orbiting
軌道を回り始めた
coalesce
合体する
theory 説

Pair Work　下線部が何を指しているかパートナーと一緒に考えましょう。

True or False

本文の内容と一致すれば **T** (True) を、一致しなければ **F** (False) を記入しましょう。

( ) 1. Stargazing is a nice pastime for dreamers.

( ) 2. Scientists are not certain of the origin of the Moon.

( ) 3. There are several possible scenarios to explain the Moon's existence.

( ) 4. The most likely scenario is that the Moon came from near Jupiter.

( ) 5. Theia and Gaia were about the same size.

( ) 6. Gaia and Theia became one planet, our Earth.

( ) 7. The Moon was made from material from the collision.

( ) 8. Scientists want more moon rocks.

Comprehension Questions

本文を読んで以下の質問に日本語で答えましょう。

1. 月は何年前に誕生しましたか。

2. 月の誕生についていくつの仮説が述べられていますか。それぞれ説明してみましょう。

3. 上記の仮説のうち、どれが一番もっともらしいとされていますか。それはなぜですか。

Collocation

日本語をヒントに空欄を埋め意味の通る英文にしましょう。

1. She is **blessed** (   ) a nice family and many good friends. 「～に恵まれている」

2. The vase **split** (   ) two pieces when he dropped it. 「～に分かれた」

3. Wine is **made** (   ) grapes. 「～でできている」

4. While cooking, water is **absorbed** (   ) rice to make it moist and sticky.

　　　　　　　　　　　　　　　　　　　　　　　　　　　　　　　　　「～に吸収された」

5. These footprints are important **evidence** (   ) this crime. 「～を示す証拠」

Unit 8

Reading Summary

下記の日本語をヒントにして空欄に当てはまる語（1語とは限りません）を入れ、本文の要約を完成させましょう。必要なら辞書を使いましょう。

Stargazing is a pleasant way to spend time. We can sometimes enjoy amazing (　　　　　　) such as observing a blood moon. However, the origin of the Moon is still a mystery. Scientists have considered several different (　　　　　　), and among them one seems most likely. This hypothesis states that (　　　　　　) there were two planets, Gaia and Theia. They both orbited the Sun, but Theia's orbit was (　　　　　　). (　　　　　　) it smashed into Gaia. This huge collision created a lot of debris, and Theia was absorbed into Gaia. The Earth we know today (　　　　　　) in this way. After some time, the debris circulating the Earth coalesced to (　　　　　　) the Moon. Scientists have looked for (　　　　　　) to support this (　　　　　　) from the moon rocks brought back by the Apollo missions. Now they want more moon rocks, so perhaps a new mission to the Moon should be (　　　　　　).

仮説	結局のところ	現象	形作られた	形作る
証拠	説	何十億年前に	打ち上げる	不安定な

Grammar Point + Grammar Exercise

現在分詞と過去分詞の働きの１つ

・名詞を修飾し、それぞれ「～している」「～される」という意味になる
・修飾語句を伴うと名詞の後に置かれる

I have a friend underline{working in the USA}.
Who is that girl underline{sitting on the sofa over there}?
The Moon was an object underline{captured by the Earth's gravity}.
Rocks underline{found on the Moon} are important for scientists.

（　）内の動詞の原形を現在分詞または過去分詞に変えて意味の通る英文を完成させましょう。

1. They have found the (hide) money.
2. Don't wake up a (sleep) baby.
3. What is the language (speak) in Sweden?
4. Who is that woman (study) in the library every evening?
5. She finally decided to buy a (use) car.

Unit 9 Road Rage

Vocabulary Task 🎧 25-26

下記の語の意味を辞書で確認しましょう。

scary	encountered	minor	error
stress	installed	route	vehicles

空欄に上記の語を入れて意味の通る英文にしましょう。

1. Children do not like hearing _____ stories at night.

2. I _____ an elephant on a safari.

3. His problem is a _____ one compared to mine.

4. I only made one _____ on my English test.

5. She _____ a new air conditioner in her apartment.

6. Bicycles, cars, buses and airplanes are _____.

7. The taxi took the shortest _____ to the hotel.

8. Doctors suffer greatly from _____.

上記の語を本文中から見つけて○をつけましょう。

NOTES

1 Getting a driver's license is a priority for many college students, despite the high cost.

2 After passing the driving test, the first few times driving alone on roads can be scary. There are many things to be aware of and many dangers to avoid.

3 Recently, according to news stories, there is one more danger that we might encounter when driving — road **rage**.

rage
激怒

4 In English, rage means extreme anger. Road rage is when one driver gets very angry with another driver and then starts to do dangerous things.

5 Consider a road rage incident between two drivers, Driver A and Driver B. Driver A is in front and makes a minor error. This makes Driver B very angry. Driver B starts to drive dangerously. He starts **tailgating** Driver A. Then he **overtakes** Driver A and suddenly **slams on the brakes**. Driver A must also **brake** suddenly. Driver B starts **swerving** and braking. Finally he stops his car, gets out and tries to attack Driver A.

tailgate
前車にピッタリついて
運転する、あおり運転
する
overtake
〜を追い越す
slam on the brakes
急ブレーキをかける
brake
ブレーキをかける
swerve
それる、急に向きをか
える

6 As we can see, a road rager such as Driver B can be a very dangerous person.

7 Why do people get road rage? One explanation might be stress. They have stress in their lives or else they feel stress when driving. Alternatively, some people may be naturally aggressive and become even more aggressive when driving.

8 Fortunately, new technology can help protect us against road ragers. Some people install **dashcams**, which make video recordings of the road in front and behind.

dashcam
ドライブレコーダー

9 How should people deal with road ragers? Firstly, never get angry yourself. Slow down and drive safely. If possible, stop your car or else change your route. Never make eye contact with the road rager. If he gets out of his vehicle and approaches your vehicle, close the windows and lock the doors. Never speak to or try to fight with the road rager. If you have stopped, call the police on your smartphone.

(317 words)

 **Pair Work**　下線部が何を指しているかパートナーと一緒に考えましょう。

True or False

本文の内容と一致すれば **T** (True) を、一致しなければ **F** (False) を記入しましょう。

( ) 1. Few students want to get a driver's license these days.

( ) 2. Road rage means getting very angry when driving.

( ) 3. Sometimes a road rager may try to attack another driver.

( ) 4. Some road ragers probably have stress in their lives.

( ) 5. Aggressive people might become more aggressive when driving.

( ) 6. All cars must install dashcams by law.

( ) 7. In a road rage incident, it is a good idea to find a different route.

( ) 8. Speaking with the road rager is the best way to resolve the situation.

Comprehension Questions

本文を読んで以下の質問に日本語で答えましょう。

1. road rage とは何ですか。

2. road rage の原因は何ですか。

3. road ragers の対処法についてどのように述べられていますか。

Collocation

日本語をヒントに空欄を埋め意味の通る英文にしましょう。

1. In my company, we must be **aware** (　　　) our customers' needs. 「～に気づく」

2. **According** (　　　) the weather forecast, it will rain tomorrow. 「～によると」

3. My father often **gets angry** (　　　) my younger brother. 「～に憤る」

4. This software will **protect** our computers (　　　) computer viruses and hackers. 「～から守る」

5. During a presentation, always **make eye contact** (　　　) the audience.

「～と目を合わせる」

Reading Summary

下記の日本語をヒントにして空欄に当てはまる語（1語とは限りません）を入れ、本文の要約を完成させましょう。必要なら辞書を使いましょう。

Young people are eager to get a driver's license but there are many things we must be (　　　　　　　) when driving. One thing we must definitely try to (　　　　　　) is a road rage incident. Some drivers cannot control themselves and get extremely angry, even over (　　　　　　　) things. These road ragers then try to intimidate other drivers. They (　　　　　　) and, in the worst cases, may even (　　　　　　) other drivers. Some of their dangerous driving techniques include tailgating, swerving and braking suddenly. There is no excuse for their behavior, but it may be (　　　　　　　) in their lives or aggression. It is a good idea to (　　　　　) a dashcam in your car to record (　　　　　　　) in case of a road rage incident. If you do encounter a road rager, stay calm and drive safely. Avoid (　　　　　　　) the road rager and if he (　　　　　　) your car, close the window and lock the doors. Call the police by all means.

危険運転をする	攻撃する	避ける	証拠	ストレスが原因の
設置する	小さな	近づく	注意する	～と目を合わせること

Grammar Point + Grammar Exercise

つなぎの言葉②

対立を表す despite の使い方

despite の後には名詞、または名詞に代わるものを置く

Getting a driver's license is a priority for many college students, **despite** the high cost.

理由を表す because of の使い方

because of の後には名詞、または名詞に代わるものを置く

People get road rage **because of** stress in their lives.

despite または because of を使用して意味のとおる英文を完成させましょう。

1．We didn't play tennis (　　　　　　　) rain.
2．I failed the test (　　　　　　) my hard work.
3．You will flunk the course (　　　　　　) your absences.
4．He went to school (　　　　　　) his sickness.
5．He was fired (　　　　　) laziness.

Irritating Things on the Train

Vocabulary Task

🎧 28-29

下記の語の意味を辞書で確認しましょう。

commute	irritating	summarized	removed
obstructs	ignored	inevitable	source

空欄に上記の語を入れて意味の通る英文にしましょう。

1. He _____ all the glasses from the table.

2. If we continue like this, global warming is _____.

3. They _____ to the office by train every morning.

4. He _____ me at the party.

5. His car often _____ the sidewalk. He should park it in a different place.

6. The content of the report is _____ in her email.

7. Not being able to speak English was the _____ of his trouble.

8. It is _____ to wait in a long line.

上記の語を本文中から見つけて○をつけましょう。

Unit 10

Reading

🎧 30

1 Many young college students spend time every day commuting by train.

2 For some people, this time is a good chance to take a nap. For others, it might be valuable time for **texting**, watching YouTube or listening to music. And for very **diligent** students, commuting provides a chance for extra study.

3 **Whichever way we choose** to spend the time on the train, it is an unfortunate fact that some things irritate us during the journey.

4 To find out the most irritating things on the train, we surveyed a group of about 50 college students in the Tokyo area. Their answers are summarized below.

5 One common **irritant** was people using **rucksacks**. Some people do not remove <u>them</u> when entering the train. <u>They</u> **bash** or obstruct the people behind <u>them</u> with the rucksack and do not seem to care.

6 Another irritating behavior that some survey participants mentioned was people cutting in line on the platform and then **dashing** for an empty seat. It might be rare but when it does happen, it is very annoying.

7 And how about if someone falls asleep on your shoulder? That was a common complaint in the survey. This is an awkward situation to deal with. Should we pretend to ignore <u>it</u> or make a sudden movement to try to wake the person up?

8 Being pushed also seems to irritate many people. During the rush hour of course there will be some pushing — <u>that</u> is inevitable. But some people tend to push too much. Perhaps they want to give <u>themselves</u> an extra bit of space. <u>It</u> seems selfish.

9 Finally, one surprising complaint was about perfume. For some of our participants, it seems that people wearing perfume are a source of irritation. Obviously, a perfume <u>that</u> smells nice for one person may be too strong for another.

10 How about you? What kinds of things irritate you on the train?

(312 words)

Pair Work 下線部が何を指しているかパートナーと一緒に考えましょう。

---

text
携帯でメッセージを送る
diligent
勤勉な
whichever way we choose
どのような方法を選ぶにしても

irritant
不快にさせるもの
rucksack
リュックサック
bash
強く打つ

dash
突進する

True or False

本文の内容と一致すれば **T**（True）を、一致しなければ **F**（False）を記入しましょう。

（　）1．Texting is the most popular commuting activity.

（　）2．Studying on the train is not allowed.

（　）3．Students from all over Japan participated in the survey.

（　）4．Baggage was one category that caused irritation.

（　）5．It seems that some people are unable to line up on the platform.

（　）6．Falling asleep on someone's shoulder is no problem.

（　）7．If you push too much on the train, people get irritated.

（　）8．Perfume was mentioned as the number one source of irritation.

Comprehension Questions

本文を読んで以下の質問に日本語で答えましょう。

1．通学中の電車の中で何ができますか。

2．通学中の電車の中で起こりうる嫌なことはいくつ述べられていますか。

3．嫌なことそれぞれを説明してみましょう。

Collocation

日本語をヒントに空欄を埋め意味の通る英文にしましょう。

1．I usually（　　　　）**a nap** after lunch.　「昼寝をする」

2．Traveling abroad provides **a chance**（　　　）practicing English.　「〜の機会」

3．A man **cut**（　　　）**line** at the supermarket checkout yesterday.　「列に割り込む」

4．My classmate often（　　　　　　）during lessons.　「眠り込む」

5．This situation is difficult. I don't know how to **deal**（　　　　　）it.　「処理する・対処する」

Reading Summary

下記の日本語をヒントにして空欄に当てはまる語（1語とは限りません）を入れ、本文の要約を完成させましょう。必要なら辞書を使いましょう。

People spend time in various ways on the train but (   ) they also (   ) many things that are (   ). To gain an understanding of what is irritating, a survey was conducted among college students in Tokyo. The results identified which irritating things were most commonly mentioned by the (   ). One (   ) of irritation was found to be people using rucksacks. Such people often hit other people with the rucksack and (   ) get in the way. Another irritant is people who do not line up properly and then try to grab vacant seats before other people. (   ), a person who (   ) on another person's shoulder might be considered irritating by other train users. It might be a difficult situation to (   ). Other sources of irritation (   ) people who push others too much within the train and also people who put on perfume or cologne.

扱う	いらいらさせる	加えて	原因	参加者	
〜しがちである	遭遇する	近づく	不運にも	含む	寝入る

Grammar Point + Grammar Exercise

〜 ing, 〜 ed で終わる形容詞

There might be many things that are **irritating** when commuting by train.
You sometimes get **irritated** at a passenger's behavior on the train.

(　) の中の動詞を適切な形容詞に変えて意味の通る英文にしましょう。

1. I got very (exhaust) after being on the rush-hour train for a long time.
2. He looked (bore) after waiting for his friend for two hours.
3. I heard the (surprise) news.
4. Everyone got (surprise) at the news.
5. I felt more (terrify) than ever.

Unit 11 Live Action Versions of Animated Movies

Vocabulary Task

🎧 31-32

下記の語の意味を辞書で確認しましょう。

| adaptation | classic | generated | imagery |
| released | update | undermined | appeal |

空欄に上記の語を入れて意味の通る英文にしましょう。

1. The TV station will _____ us on the typhoon's progress.

2. I do not understand the _____ of playing video games.

3. When was Elton John's first record _____?

4. The rumors _____ the president's credibility.

5. The Grudge is a Hollywood _____ of the Japanese movie, Ju-On.

6. *The Old Man and the Sea* is a _____ work of fiction.

7. Heat is _____ by the human body.

8. A lot of dark _____ was used in this horror film.

上記の語を本文中から見つけて○をつけましょう。

Reading

NOTES

1 The list of Disney **hand-drawn animated movies** is long, stretching from **Snow White and the Seven Dwarfs** released in 1937, to **The Princess and the Frog** released in 2009.

2 These days, however, most of Disney's animated movies are not hand drawn. Titles such as Toy Story, Monsters Inc., **Frozen** and many others are created by using computers.

3 But now there is a new trend. Disney is making live-action adaptations of the classic hand-drawn Disney movies. **Beauty and the Beast** (2017), Dumbo (2019) and Mulan (2020) are all examples of such remakes.

4 There are two types of live-action remakes. One type has human actors <u>who</u> interact with computer-generated characters and imagery. Beauty and the Beast is an example. The other type looks like live action but is, in fact, **photorealistic computer animation**. The Lion King (2019) is an example of <u>this</u> type of remake.

5 Why is Disney releasing live-action remakes of <u>its</u> classic movies?

6 There may be several reasons.

7 First, live-action remakes are a good way to "**reboot**" the classic hand-drawn animated movies, but in a new way. Recreating the same movie again with updated animation would be boring and might **undermine** the appeal of the original movie.

8 Second, the original hand-drawn Disney movies might seem a little old-fashioned for today's children. A live-action remake can make the movie seem fresh and modern.

9 One more reason is that famous stars can be used in live-action movies. Of course, there are many wonderful **voice actors** in animated movies but, to be frank, <u>they</u> are behind the scenes. The animated characters are the stars.

10 In contrast, Beauty and the Beast had a major star—Emma Watson. She is famous for her role in the Harry Potter movies and is very popular, especially among young girls. Her appearance in Beauty and the Beast surely helped <u>that</u> movie to become successful.

(306 words)

---

hand-drawn animated movie
手描きのアニメ映画
（セルアニメ）
Snow White and the Seven Dwarfs
白雪姫
The Princess and the Frog
プリンセスと魔法のキス
Frozen
アナと雪の女王
Beauty and the Beast
美女と野獣

photorealistic computer animation
写実的なコンピュータアニメ映画

reboot
再起動する

undermine
損ねる

voice actor
声優

 Pair Work　下線部が何を指しているかパートナーと一緒に考えましょう。

True or False

本文の内容と一致すれば **T** (True) を、一致しなければ **F** (False) を記入しましょう。

( ) 1. Snow White and the Seven Dwarfs was released before WW2.

( ) 2. Frozen is a computer-generated animated movie.

( ) 3. The original Dumbo movie has been remade as a live-action movie.

( ) 4. There seems to be two kinds of live-action remakes.

( ) 5. There is one main reason for Disney releasing live-action remakes.

( ) 6. Disney seems to want to reboot its old hand-drawn animated movies.

( ) 7. These days, children prefer the old-fashioned animated movies.

( ) 8. It is best to use unknown actors for live-action remakes.

Comprehension Questions

本文を読んで以下の質問に日本語で答えましょう。

1. ディズニー映画の最近のトレンドは何ですか。

2. なぜディズニーは昔のアニメ映画を実写の手法でリメークするのでしょうか。

3. エマ・ワトソンを映画に起用することでどのような利点がありましたか。

Collocation

日本語をヒントに空欄を埋め意味の通る英文にしましょう。

1. Japan (　　　　　　) **from** Hokkaido **to** Okinawa.　「〜から〜まで広がっている」

2. This song was **created** (　　) artificial intelligence (AI).　「〜によって作られる」

3. **To be** (　　　　), the quality of this item is not good.　「はっきり言わせてもらえば」

4. They worked hard (　　　　　) **the scenes** to make the event a success.

「舞台裏で」

5. Winters are cold in Japan. (　　　) **contrast**, summers are hot and humid.

「その一方」

Reading Summary

下記の日本語をヒントにして空欄に当てはまる語（1語とは限りません）を入れ、本文の要約を完成させましょう。必要なら辞書を使いましょう。

Disney has a long history of making hand-drawn animated movies. Some of these movies, such as Beauty and the Beast, are now being remade as live-action movies. （　　　　　） there are two kinds of live-action movies. In one type, real actors （　　　　　） and there are also CGI effects. In another type, computer animation is used to produce extremely （　　　　　） scenes. The following reasons can help to explain why live-action movies are being made these days. Firstly, a live-action movie can help to "reboot" an old （　　　　　）, without being an exact copy. Secondly, live-action movies can make older movies seem fresh and modern. This might be important to （　　　　　） interest from young children. （　　　　　）, live-action movies can use popular actors, （　　　　　） Emma Watson. This can （　　　　　） their （　　　　　） and indeed the live-action version of Beauty and the Beast was a （　　　　　）.

基本的に	現実的な	さらに	大ヒット	登場する
引き付ける	増やす	魅力	名作の映画	～のような

Grammar Point + Grammar Exercise

例示の仕方

Titles **such as** Toy Story, Monsters Inc. and Frozen are created by using computers. Beauty and the Beast (2017), Dumbo (2019) and Mulan (2020) are **all examples** of such remakes.
The Lion King (2019) is **an example of** this type of remake.

和文を参照して空欄に語（句）を入れて英文を完成させましょう。

1. Beauty and the Beast is (　　　　　　　　　) this type.
   「美女と野獣」がこのタイプの例だ。

2. She visited several countries in Europe, (　　　　　　　　　) Italy and Spain. 彼女はヨーロッパの国々、例えばイタリアやスペインなどを訪れた。

3. I like to study languages, (　　　　　　) Italian.
   私はイタリア語のような言語を学びたい。

4. He has a lot of pets, (　　　　　　) dogs, cats, snakes, turtles and tropical fish. 彼は、犬、猫、蛇、亀、熱帯魚などを含む多くのペットを飼っている。

5. I want to go abroad, (　　　　　　　　　), to Spain and Portugal.
   私は例えば、スペインやポルトガルのような外国に行きたい。

Tapioca and Bubble Tea

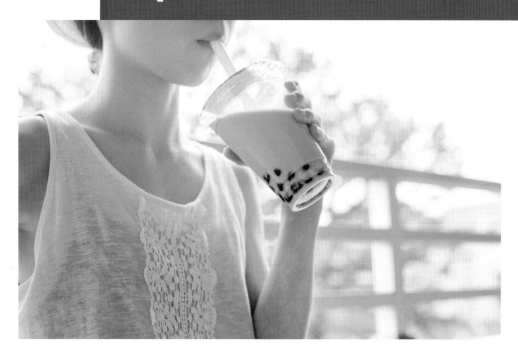

Vocabulary Task

34-35

下記の語（句）の意味を辞書で確認しましょう。

root	raw	poisonous	invented
up to	stirred	reduce	fussy

空欄に上記の語（句）を入れて意味の通る英文にしましょう。

1. He _____ his tea with a spoon.

2. Some mushrooms are _____ to humans.

3. Japanese people are _____ about the taste of ramen.

4. Thomas Edison _____ the first successful light bulb.

5. I like eating _____ vegetables.

6. Building a new road will _____ traffic jams.

7. I have to decide my future. It's _____ me.

8. The part of the plant below ground is called the _____.

上記の語（句）を本文中から見つけて○をつけましょう。

Reading

NOTES

1 **Bubble tea** is a drink <u>that</u> has recently become popular worldwide. This beverage is tea with milk and **tapioca balls**, <u>which</u> are usually called **tapioca pearls** or "**boba**".

2 In English, the word "tapioca" does not mean bubble tea. Tapioca is actually the **starch** powder made from the roots of the **cassava** plant. It is important to make <u>this</u> powder carefully, because raw cassava roots are poisonous. To prepare boba we add water and sugar to the powder and make a **dough**. This is cut into small pieces and boiled.

3 Bubble tea was invented in Taiwan in the 1980s. Tearooms in Taiwan started adding tapioca pearls to tea and the drink became popular. Originally, white tapioca pearls were used. However, by adding **brown sugar**, the pearls become black (actually dark brown) and now <u>these</u> are most commonly used in bubble tea.

4 Bubble tea is a fun beverage! Most people like to drink the tea and eat the pearls at the same time. Bubble tea is usually served with a big straw, so we can easily suck up tea and tapioca pearls together. It is a good idea to stir the bubble tea often, otherwise the pearls might stick together at the bottom of the glass.

5 If you want to leave some of the tapioca pearls, <u>that</u> is OK. <u>It</u> is up to you. One point is that bubble tea is pretty high in calories. There is sugar in the tea and the tapioca pearls are basically starch and sugar. If you leave some pearls, you can reduce the calories.

6 These days, bubble tea fans are becoming fussy. <u>They</u> demand new flavors and unique combinations of tea and boba. Some specialist bubble tea shops make <u>their</u> own boba in-store and customers have a choice of boba flavors, such as strawberry or **purple yam**.

7 Colorful combinations of tea and boba are perfect for **posting to Instagram**!

(312 words)

Bubble tea
バブルティー、タピオカティー
tapioca ball
キャサバの根から抽出したデンプンであるタピオカの製品
tapioca pearl
タピオカパール（バブルティー中の粒）
boba
ボバ（中国語の波羅茶に由来）
starch
デンプン
cassava
キャサバ（イモノキ属の熱帯低木）
dough
生地
brown sugar
黒糖

purple yam
紅いも
post to Instagram
インスタに載せる

 Pair Work 　下線部が何を指しているかパートナーと一緒に考えましょう。

True or False

本文の内容と一致すれば **T** (True) を、一致しなければ **F** (False) を記入しましょう。

(　) 1．Tapioca balls are also called tapioca globes.

(　) 2．Cassava roots are used to make tapioca.

(　) 3．Bubble tea was first made in Europe.

(　) 4．Black tapioca pearls contain brown sugar.

(　) 5．Most people drink the tea first and then have the pearls.

(　) 6．Stirring bubble tea helps to prevent the pearls sticking together.

(　) 7．Tapioca balls have zero calories.

(　) 8．Fruit-flavored tapioca pearls are available.

Comprehension Questions

本文を読んで以下の質問に日本語で答えましょう。

1．タピオカの原料は何ですか。

2．タピオカはいつどこで初めて作られましたか。

3．タピオカドリンクのファンは最近何を求めていますか。

Collocation

日本語をヒントに空欄を埋め意味の通る英文にしましょう。

1．This cocktail is always **served** (　　　　) a slice of lemon. 「～と一緒に出される」

2．Butterflies **suck** (　　) nectar from flowers. 「～を吸い上げる」

3．Pasta sometimes **sticks** (　　　　) when cooking. 「くっつく」

4．She found the photo (　　) **the bottom of** an old box. 「～の底に」

5．Margarine is **high** (　　) fat. 「～が多い」

Reading Summary

下記の日本語をヒントにして空欄に当てはまる語（１語とは限りません）を入れ、本文の要約を完成させましょう。必要なら辞書を使いましょう。

Tapioca pearls or "boba" are one of the main ingredients in bubble tea. They are (   ) tapioca starch powder which comes from the roots of cassava plants. These roots are poisonous so must (   ) carefully. Several decades ago in Taiwan, tearoom owners (   ) tapioca pearls to tea and a new drink was born. It became a big hit in Taiwan and then (   ) worldwide. Bubble tea looks attractive and is fun to drink. Most shops serve bubble tea with a big straw so that customers can (   ) tea and tapioca pearls (   ). Although it is a delicious drink, (   ) should be aware that it is quite (   ). To (   ) the calories we can leave some of the pearls at the bottom of the glass. For people who really love bubble tea, there is some good news. Recently, gourmet bubble tea shops have (   ) and are selling boba with new flavors.

カロリーが高い	加えた	消費者	吸う	出現した
～で作られた	同時に	加工される	減らす	広がった

Grammar Point + Grammar Exercise

時や場所を表す前置詞 at, on, in

Bubble tea has become popular around the world **in** the past few years.
Bubble tea was invented **in** the 1980s.

The cassava plant is now grown **in** many tropical countries.
There is sugar **in** the tea.
A chain of bubble tea shops started **in** Taiwan.

和文を参考にして空欄に適切な前置詞（at / on / in）を入れましょう。

1. Shaved ice sells well (   ) the summer.　かき氷は夏によく売れる。
2. He often drinks bubble tea (   ) the evening.　彼は夕方によくタピオカティーを飲む。
3. I live (   ) the 7th floor of this building.　私はこのビルの７階に住んでます。
4. My sister teaches English (   ) a high school (   ) Kobe City.
   私の姉は神戸市の高校で英語の教師をしている。
5. I usually get up (   ) 6 (   ) weekdays.　平日はたいてい６時に起床する。

Animal Beauty Contests

Vocabulary Task

🎧 37-38

下記の語の意味を辞書で確認しましょう。

| individuals | nominated | candidates | voted |
| period | comment | promotes | destination |

空欄に上記の語を入れて意味の通る英文にしましょう。

1. Exercising _____ health.

2. According to the news, six _____ were injured in the accident.

3. Last year, I _____ in an election for the first time.

4. We _____ three athletes to be members of the Olympic team.

5. We finally reached our _____ after a long flight.

6. The students will be on vacation for a _____ of two months.

7. The two presidential _____ will speak on TV tonight.

8. If you have finished talking, may I make a _____?

上記の語を本文中から見つけて〇をつけましょう。

NOTES

1 Human beauty contests such as Miss World and Mr. Universe are well known. Indeed, many colleges in Japan hold a "Miss" or "Mr." contest during their school festivals.

2 However, these days, animal beauty contests are gaining popularity. Such contests are not only for cute cats and dogs. Around the world, we can find a Miss Cow contest, a Miss Camel contest and even a Miss (or Mr.) **Tarantula** contest.

3 Recently, a new animal beauty contest was held in Australia. The goal was to find the country's cutest koala and seventy contestants **entered**.

4 The rules of the contest **stipulated** that only **joeys** (young koalas) living in Australia could enter. Both **wildlife** parks and individuals could nominate koala candidates, simply by sending an email with three photos.

5 From the seventy submissions, a **shortlist** of thirteen cute joeys was decided and the photos were then **posted** on Facebook. People could view the photos and choose their favorite candidate by clicking "Like" or "Love". During the 24-hour voting period, thousands of people voted and the winner was decided.

6 Tallow, an eight-month-old joey was voted the cutest young koala in Australia. She lives at Paradise Country, an animal park on the **Gold Coast** near **Brisbane**, and has now become a star attraction there. In the comments, voters said that they loved her big brown eyes, big cute nose and **fluffy** ears.

7 The event was organized by Tourism Australia, a **government agency** with **responsibility** for promoting Australia as a tourist destination. The contest was fun and also a great way to advertise many wildlife parks around Australia. In addition, because the story was picked up by the media worldwide, it helped to promote Australia as a tourist destination.

8 What kind of animal beauty contest could promote tourism in your country?

(292 words)

tarantula
オオツチグモ科の大型のクモ

enter
コンテストの募集に応じる

stipulate
規定する

joey
有袋動物の子

wildlife
野生生物

shortlist
選抜候補者名簿

post
掲示する

Gold Coast
オーストラリアにある観光都市

Brisbane
オーストラリアのクイーンズランド州の州都

fluffy
ふわふわした

government agency
政府機関

responsibility
責任

 **Pair Work** 下線部が何を指しているかパートナーと一緒に考えましょう。

True or False

本文の内容と一致すれば **T** (True) を、一致しなければ **F** (False) を記入しましょう。

(　) 1 ． Miss World is an example of a famous beauty pageant.

(　) 2 ． Animal beauty contests have become more popular than human ones.

(　) 3 ． Over one hundred joeys entered the koala contest.

(　) 4 ． Only entries from within Australia were accepted.

(　) 5 ． Social media was used to choose the winner of the koala contest.

(　) 6 ． Voting was limited to koala owners.

(　) 7 ． Tallow, a koala living in the wild near Brisbane, was the winner.

(　) 8 ． Tourism Australia aims to promote Australia as a travel destination.

Comprehension Questions

本文を読んで以下の質問に日本語で答えましょう。

1 ． アニマル・ビューティー・コンテストの例をあげましょう。

2 ． オーストラリアで行われたコアラのコンテストの出場条件は何ですか。

3 ． そのコンテストで優勝したコアラはどのように決定されましたか。

Collocation

日本語をヒントに空欄を埋め意味の通る英文にしましょう。

1 ． We will (　 　 　) a photo **contest** during our school festival. 「コンテストを開催する」

2 ． **Thousands** (　 　) bears live in Japan's forests. 「何千もの〜」

3 ． The orangutan is the **star attraction** (　 　) that zoo. 「〜での客寄せ」

4 ． Our end-of-year party will **be organized** (　 　) Mr. Sato this year.

「〜によって組織される」

5 ． You can see a panda at Ueno Zoo. (　 　) **addition**, there is a polar bear. 「加えて」

Reading Summary

下記の日本語をヒントにして空欄に当てはまる語（1語とは限りません）を入れ、本文の要約を完成させましょう。必要なら辞書を使いましょう。

Most people are (　　　　　　　) with famous beauty contests and also local ones such as those held on college campuses in Japan. Recently, animal beauty contests have been (　　　　　　) worldwide and several unusual contests have been reported in the media. In Australia, a contest was held to try to find the cutest koala joey in the country. Many entries were received and the shortlisted (　　　　　　) had their photographs uploaded to a social networking site. People could access the website and choose their (　　　　) koala. Although it must have been difficult to choose (　　　　) the candidates, a joey called Tallow (　　　　) as the (　　　　　). She is kept at an animal park near Brisbane and now many people are visiting the park to see Tallow. The organization that (　　　　), Tourism Australia, was able to (　　　　　) tourism in Australia (　　　) the event.

一番お気に入りの	選ばれた	候補者	コンテストを開催した	優勝者
～に精通している	促進する	人気を博している	～のお陰で	～の間で

Grammar Point + Grammar Exercise

接続詞 as の様々な意味

〈時〉　～するときに、～したとたん、～しながら

〈理由〉～なので、～だから

〈譲歩〉～だけれども　※形容詞［副詞・名詞］＋ as ＋主語＋動詞

〈比例〉～につれて

〈様態〉～と同様に、～のように

次の英文を日本語に訳しましょう。

1. As she is a nurse, she has to work carefully and accurately.
2. As you know, they contributed to the success of our experiment.
3. As I unlock the door, my cat rushes to the entrance.
4. Rich as he was, he felt so lonely.
5. As the sea level fell, the path to the small island appeared.

Vocabulary Task

🎧 40-41

下記の語の意味を辞書で確認しましょう。

energy	essential	prefers	content
obviously	similar	concern	advisable

空欄に上記の語を入れて意味の通る英文にしましょう。

1. Flour is an _____ ingredient for making bread.

2. Internet safety is a _____ for many people these days.

3. Her handwriting is _____ to mine.

4. What is the _____ of vitamin C in this supplement?

5. In Japan, it is _____ to prepare items for an emergency.

6. Look at those dark clouds! It's _____ going to rain soon.

7. Running fast takes a lot of _____.

8. Among the various movie genres, Haruma _____ SF movies.

上記の語を本文中から見つけて○をつけましょう。

Reading

 42

1 For many young people these days, particularly young men, energy drinks are an essential part of <u>their</u> lifestyle.

2 In America, the top three best-selling energy drinks are Red Bull, Monster, and Rockstar. In Japan, Rockstar is not available, but Red Bull and Monster are popular.

3 Red Bull is perhaps the most famous energy drink **worldwide**. This drink orginally comes from Thailand, <u>where</u> it is called "**Krating Daeng**." Krating means **gaur**, <u>which</u> is a kind of **bison**, and daeng means "red". Many visitors to Thailand like to try Krating Daeng.

4 Young men sometimes ask each other, "Which do you prefer, Red Bull or Monster?" <u>Some</u> prefer the smaller size of the standard Red Bull can. <u>They</u> say that Red Bull can be drunk quickly. Other people prefer the sweeter taste of Monster. <u>They</u> say that Red Bull tastes **slightly bitter**.

5 Parents worry about the caffeine content in energy drinks. Is <u>it</u> too high? In Japan, the amount of caffeine in both Red Bull and Monster is about 40mg per 100ml. Obviously, if you drink a larger can, you get more caffeine, but generally speaking, the caffeine level in an energy drink is similar to a cup of coffee.

6 We also see mysterious words on energy drink cans, such as "**taurine**" or "**arginine**." What are <u>these</u>? To some people, <u>they</u> may sound unhealthy.

7 Actually, taurine and arginine are just **amino acids**. <u>They</u> occur naturally in the body and may improve performance in sports and daily life. Most scientists think <u>they</u> are safe.

8 Rather than caffeine and amino acids, perhaps the main concern about energy drinks is that <u>they</u> are high in sugar. These days, young people's diets contain more sugar than ever before, and energy drinks can add a lot of sugar to the daily total. In view of <u>these</u> points, a limit of one can per day might be advisable.

(309 words)

worldwide
世界中で
Krating Daeng
グラティンデーン
gaur
ガウル（ウシ科の動物）
bison
バイソン（ウシ科の動物）

slightly bitter
少し苦めで

taurine
タウリン（アミノ酸の一種）
arginin
アルギニン（アミノ酸の一種）
amino acid
アミノ酸

Pair Work　下線部が何を指しているかパートナーと一緒に考えましょう。

True or False

本文の内容と一致すれば **T** (True) を、一致しなければ **F** (False) を記入しましょう。

( )１. Energy drinks are popular, especially among young women.

( )２. Rockstar is currently sold in shops in Japan.

( )３. Red Bull originated in Thailand.

( )４. The Thai name for Red Bull has a completely different meaning.

( )５. Monster is considered to be sweeter than Red Bull.

( )６. Red Bull has much less caffeine per 100ml than Monster.

( )７. Arginine is an amino acid found in energy drinks.

( )８. The sugar content in energy drinks is low.

Comprehension Questions

本文を読んで以下の質問に日本語で答えましょう。

１. アメリカで販売されている三大エナジードリンクは何ですか。

２. 世界中で最も有名なエナジードリンクは何ですか。

３. 若者がエナジードリンクを飲むことに関しての懸念は何ですか。

Collocation

日本語をヒントに空欄を埋め意味の通る英文にしましょう。

１.（　　　　　）**days**, young people use social media a lot. 「最近」

２. Worcester sauce originally **comes**（　　　　　）England. 「～からのものである」

３. During the pairwork activity, please ask（　　　　　）**other** questions. 「互いに」

４.（　　　　　）**speaking**, American people are friendly and talkative.

「一般的に言って」

５. **In**（　　　　　）**of** the bad economic situation, we must save money. 「を考えると」

Reading Summary

下記の日本語をヒントにして空欄に当てはまる語（1語とは限りません）を入れ、本文の要約を完成させましょう。必要なら辞書を使いましょう。

Young people, especially young men, (   ) drink a lot of energy drinks these days. This is a (   ) trend now, and brands such as Red Bull, Monster and Rockstar are sold in many countries. In Japan, the two most (   ) non-Japanese energy drinks are Red Bull and Monster. Red Bull (   ) in Thailand. The (   ) version is still sold there and is called Krating Daeng. Comparing Red Bull and Monster, some people like Red Bull for its smaller size, (   ) other people like Monster for its sweeter taste. They (   ) have a similar caffeine content per 100ml and are in fact quite (   ) coffee in the (   ) of caffeine contained. Other common ingredients are amino acids and sugar. Because the sugar content in energy drinks is high, people may want to limit their (   ) to one can per day.

一方では	元の	～する傾向にある	世界的な	摂取量
～と同様の	両方とも	始まった	普通の	量

Grammar Point + Grammar Exercise

used to と be(get) used to の違い

■ （現在と比較して）～したものだった・以前は～だった【to のあとには動詞の原形】
Now it is not available, but Rockstar **used to** *be* sold in Japan.
There **used to** *be* a big building here.
He **used to** *speak* in public.

■ ～に慣れている・～に慣れた【to のあとには名詞、または名詞に代わるもの】
He is **used to** *speaking* in public.
Mary **got used to** *getting* up early.

次の英文を日本語に訳しましょう。
1. I used to play the flute every day.
2. Did you use to wear these glasses?
3. You should get used to using a smartphone.
4. He is used to cold weather because he comes from Greenland.
5. I didn't use to play tennis.

Unit 15

Places Near to Japan That Are Good for Studying English

Vocabulary Task

43-44

下記の語の意味を辞書で確認しましょう。

provide	environment	budget	reputation
multicultural	urban	communicate	options

空欄に上記の語を入れて意味の通る英文にしましょう。

1. This _____ area has a lot of shops and offices.

2. They _____ everything for their customers.

3. He has a good _____ because he is hard-working.

4. The rain forest is a natural _____ with many animals.

5. You have two _____ for dessert.

6. As my best friend moved away, we now _____ by email.

7. The government announced the _____ for the next year.

8. People in Malaysia live in a _____ society.

上記の語を本文中から見つけて○をつけましょう。

Reading

NOTES

1 In the past, if young Japanese people planned to study English in another country, <u>they</u> would probably go to faraway places such as the United States or the United Kingdom.

2 These days, things have changed. Many locations worldwide now have good English language schools and provide a pleasant environment for learning English.

3 For young people on a limited budget, destinations nearer Japan are cheaper and quicker to get to.

4 So, what are some good places near Japan for studying English?

5 Recently, **Cebu Island** in the Philippines has become well known for <u>its</u> English schools. The flight from Japan is just five hours, local prices are reasonable and, as a bonus, <u>it</u> has beautiful beaches. One more great aspect of learning English in Cebu is that the teachers are very kind and friendly.

6 Malaysia is another popular destination for **cost-conscious** English learners. In **Kuala Lumpur** there are several English schools with good reputations. Malaysia has a multicultural society and in urban areas many people speak English. Thus there are lots of opportunities to practice English outside of class.

7 Another new location for English learners is **Fiji**. This **Pacific** island, famous for <u>its</u> beautiful sea and **coral reefs**, offers English lessons at very low prices. The **Fijian** people give a kind welcome to everybody and will happily communicate in English, even with low-level learners.

8 If you have a bigger budget but still want to study English nearer Japan, Cairns in Australia might be a good option. This small city located in the northeast of Australia is much nearer Japan than Sydney or Melbourne. <u>It</u> is a beautiful place with good weather, good security and many different outdoor activities to try.

9 Wherever you go, the advice is the same. Study hard and speak a lot of English with everyone you meet.

(298 words)

Cebu Island
セブ島（フィリピン中部のビサヤ諸島にある島）

cost-conscious
コスト意識の高い
Kuala Lumpur
クアラルンプール（マレーシアの首都）

Fiji
フィジー（300以上の島からなる南太平洋の島国）
Pacific
太平洋の
coral reefs
サンゴ礁
Fijian
フィジーの

 Pair Work　下線部が何を指しているかパートナーと一緒に考えましょう。

True or False

本文の内容と一致すれば **T**（True）を、一致しなければ **F**（False）を記入しましょう。

（　）1．Recently, the UK has become very popular as a place to learn English.

（　）2．The number of places for studying English abroad has declined.

（　）3．In Cebu, the teachers are kind but the costs are high.

（　）4．English is widely spoken in urban areas in Malaysia.

（　）5．Fiji is well known for its ocean environment.

（　）6．Fijian people are glad to speak English with learners.

（　）7．Cairns is further from Japan than Sydney.

（　）8．Cairns is known as a safe place.

Comprehension Questions

本文を読んで以下の質問に日本語で答えましょう。

1．英語を学べる場所としていくつあげられていますか。

2．マレーシアが英語学習において良い理由は何ですか。

3．ケアンズはどのような英語学習者に向いていますか。

Collocation

日本語をヒントに空欄を埋め意味の通る英文にしましょう。

1．What time will we **get （　　　）** our destination? 「到着する」

2．Japan is **well known （　　　）** its delicious food. 「～でよく知られている」

3．**Outside （　　　）** business hours, you can contact me on my cell phone. 「以外に」

4．Hawaii is **famous （　　　）** its hula dancing. 「～で有名な」

5．Taipei is **located （　　　）** the north of Taiwan. 「～に位置する」

Reading Summary

下記の日本語をヒントにして空欄に当てはまる語（1語とは限りません）を入れ、本文の要約を完成させましょう。必要なら辞書を使いましょう。

（　　　　　　） the past, Japanese students of English now have more （　　　　　　） for study abroad. （　　　　　　） spend a lot of time and money traveling to faraway places, they can learn English in （　　　　　　） nearer to Japan. Cebu Island in the Philippines is one such destination. It has become famous as an English learning center and has a lot of good schools and teachers. One （　　　　　　） that students like about Cebu is that the teachers are very kind to the students. Kuala Lumpur in Malaysia is also （　　　　　　） its English schools. （　　　　　　） studying in the school, students can practice a lot outside class. Malaysia is a （　　　　　　） so people of any nationality can fit in well there. Fiji is one of the newest options for English students who want to study abroad. Tuition costs are low and the Fijian people are friendly and welcome visitors. One more option is Cairns in north-eastern Australia. It might be more （　　　　　　） but it is a beautiful place and there are many opportunities for （　　　　　　）.

〜の他に	課外活動	〜で有名な	〜と比べると	一面
〜よりむしろ	高価な	選択肢	目的地	多文化の

Grammar Point + Grammar Exercise

Wherever, Whenever の使い方

<u>Wherever</u> you (may) go, the basic advice is always the same.

<u>Whenever</u> you (may) come, you are welcome.

Wherever または whenever を使用して次の和文を英語に訳しましょう。
1．あなたがどこにいようとあなたのことを考えている。
2．会えば必ずけんかする。
3．いつ彼に電話しても話し中だ。
4．好きなところで勉強してよい。
5．好きなところにお座りください。

著　者

Jonathan Lynch（ジョナサン・リンチ）

山本　厚子（やまもと　あつこ）

渡辺香名子（わたなべ　かなこ）

考える基礎英語読本

2021年2月20日　第1版発行

2024年3月10日　第3版発行

著　者 ── Jonathan Lynch／山本厚子／渡辺香名子

発行者 ── 前田俊秀

発行所 ── 株式会社　三修社

　　　　〒150-0001　東京都渋谷区神宮前2-2-22
　　　　TEL 03-3405-4511 ／ FAX 03-3405-4522
　　　　振替 00190-9-72758
　　　　https://www.sanshusha.co.jp
　　　　編集担当　三井るり子

印刷所 ── 倉敷印刷株式会社

©2021 Printed in Japan　ISBN978-4-384-33501-9 C1082

表紙デザイン ── SAIWAI Design（山内宏一郎）
本文デザイン・DTP ── ME TIME LLC（大貫としみ）
準拠音声制作 ── 高速録音株式会社
準拠音声録音 ── ELEC（吹込：Rachel Walzer ／ Neil DeMaere）

教科書準拠CD発売

本書の準拠CDをご希望の方は弊社までお問い合わせください。